ROAD SMARTS

Strategies
for New Drivers

CONTENTS

Skills

Driving well is a lot like being a good athlete. You have to learn to control your own reactions in order to handle a car in different situations. Focus and awareness are essential when you're behind the wheel, but foresight, anticipation, and control are skills that can be built in advance, before you're even sitting in the driver's seat.

Like an athlete, you can actually prepare yourself mentally, imagining what you would do and how you would do it when confronted with a sudden challenge. The same "mental imaging" technique that is key for athletes preparing for competition will equip you to control how you react and keep you—or get you-- out of trouble on the road. This book is designed to help with that.

The mental as well as the physical skills that make you a good driver might save your life someday, or someone else's. I guess you know that.

The Other Driver

It would be great if all your driving could be done on roads with no one else on them, but even if you go to Siberia this is not going to happen. So other drivers are key factors in any trip you make.

Rule One of driving is *don't assume anything* where other drivers are concerned. You can't count on other drivers to stop at a stop sign, stop at a red light, signal before turning, turn after signaling, or generally do all the things that make sense. You can't count on them until you actually see them doing it. Maybe the other driver isn't paying attention. Doesn't know where he's going? Is just plain ignoring the rules of the road?

Say you're at an intersection, stopped at a stop sign. Another car approaches the intersection on the crossroad, where there's also a stop sign. Is the driver going to stop? Do you know that for a fact? Maybe you think to yourself, "Sure that car's going to stop because there's a stop sign there. It's my turn and I'm just going to go." The result of this assumption may be CRASH!

Let's look at that scenario again. You're sitting at the stop sign and the other car approaches on the crossroad, where there's also a stop sign. Now you see the other car actually slowing down. You see it beginning to stop. Okay! Now you go. No crash.

And what about red lights? Sure, you've seen people run red lights. Here you are stopped at your red light and now it turns green. You've got the right of way. You've got the green light! But wait, a car is still coming on the cross road. The light is red for that car, but..... Is it coming pretty fast? Is it really going to stop? Do you know for sure?

Don't ever just count on the other driver doing the right thing. Byword: Wait till you know, then go.

The Agile Car

We hear a lot about braking time on cars: how quickly the car can come to a stop from different speeds. Of course, the faster you're going, the longer (and therefore further) it's going to take for the car to stop, even if you slam on the brakes. There are times when braking is not going to let you stop quickly enough to avoid a bad situation.

But luckily, braking is not your only option for getting out of a tough spot. And sometimes it's absolutely *not* your best option.

Suppose you're driving down a street and another car comes out of a side street right in front of you. Even if you hit the brakes hard, your car will still travel forward for quite some distance before stopping. If the other car is very close, the chances are terrific that you will not be able to stop in time and will hit the other car broadside. This could be really bad news.

But hey, cars can turn with amazing sharpness and quickness. They're designed to be able to do that. So if instead, in this situation, you turn sharply away from the other car--dodging it--you may have a much better chance of avoiding a collision. The agility of the car can save you--and the other driver, and any passengers.

Of course, you have to be sure that in turning sharply you're not going to hit another car in the lane next to you. That's one of the reasons you need to stay alert to cars around you.

And here's another important warning, if you're driving an SUV, a jeep, a van, or a pick-up. High-profile vehicles like these are more top-heavy than a car, and they don't handle the same. They can't take a sharp turn as well as a sedan and might tip over.

Know your vehicle. Find out its abilities and limitations. How agile is it? Try out some maneuvers – carefully! – in a safe area to get a good feel of the vehicle's handling.

When push comes to shove, you have more than your brakes to rely on. Brakes aren't a car's only talent. Hang onto that thought.

Overcorrecting: The Panic Response

Overcorrecting leads to a whole lot of totally unnecessary accidents, some of them fatal.

We just looked at the agility of the car and how it can help get you out of danger. But that same agility can do you in, if you use it at the wrong time!

Sound confusing? So look at this quite frequent scenario: A driver is traveling along a narrow road. Because of a momentary inattention, the car goes just a wee bit off the right side of the road, perhaps just with one front tire. Can you see this happening?

So then what? The driver quickly notices and is startled that she's a bit off the road. Yikes! She reacts (that is, over-reacts!) automatically by jerking the wheel to the left to bring the car quickly back on the road.

But the car, remember, is an agile and responsive machine. With the wheel being jerked to the left, the car goes flying to the left, crosses the center line, and heads off the other side of the road, possibly crashing into something–an approaching car, a tree, a guard rail, whatever.

Let's look a similar scenario. A driver is traveling 60 miles an hour on a four-lane highway. He's in the right-hand lane and decides to pass the car in front of him. He begins to pull out into the passing lane to his left. But OOOPS! There's a car in that lane that he didn't see at first, coming right up behind him on the left. Startled, he swings the wheel to the right to pull back into the right-hand lane. The car responds to the abrupt pull on the wheel by heading hard right, across the right-hand lane and into a guardrail or off the road. BAM. That's the panic response.

How do you avoid having these things happen to you? How do you learn to avoid the panic response?

One key thing you can do is practice. Find a big empty parking lot or a little-used back road. Drive slowly along the edge of the parking lot or road, and let the car drift just a bit to the right so it goes slightly onto the edge of the roadway. Then GENTLY bring it back. You'll discover how little it really takes to do that. Just a bit of calm readjustment of the wheel – *not* a big scared swerve. If you practice and fix in your mind how little it takes to bring the car back where you want it, teaching yourself not to panic, that knowledge will stay in your mind and it *will* be with you when you need it.

Another thing you can do is practice mentally by imagining the situation. Imagine going off the side of a road and imagine coming back gently, no panic, just the right level of correction. Doing this mental imaging a few times now and then will really help. Really! There's no need for you, a good driver, to be a victim of the panic response.

Not Going Where You're Looking

When you're passing a police car or emergency vehicle that is stopped at the side of the road, many states have a law that requires you to slow down and if possible move to the left (or into the left lane on a four-lane highway). Way too many police officers, workers, and others, standing or working by the side of a road, have been killed by cars coming along and driving right into them.

The reason this can happen, and in fact can happen easily, is the natural tendency we all have to drift in the direction we're looking. If you're looking at something on the right side of the road, your car will tend to start heading slightly to the right. You could be completely unaware this is happening, and certainly not be doing it on purpose. Of course it's not the car that's heading that way by itself, it's your steering, unconsciously following the direction of your gaze.

So how do we fix this? For one thing, it's key just to be aware this can happen. Awareness can keep you from inadvertently drifting in the direction you're looking.

Just as important, when you see an emergency vehicle – a police car, fire truck, ambulance, state highway vehicle, or tow truck stopped at the side of the road (or even someone trying to change a flat tire), slow down. If there's room, pull to the left, further away from the vehicles and the persons near them. If your state doesn't have that law, do it anyway.

The One-Second Limit

How far does a car travel in one second?

At 60 miles per hour, in one second a car travels 88 feet or almost 30 yards – one-third the length of a football field. In two seconds at 60 miles per hour, it travels a whole 60 yards.

Even at 30 miles per hour, a pretty standard speed limit for towns and suburbs, in one second a car travels 44 feet, almost 15 yards. In two seconds, twice as far.

Suppose you're going along at 60 miles per hour. You glance away from the road to fiddle with the radio, put in a new CD, try to find your cell phone that's ringing, or talk to someone else in the car. How long before you look at the road again? How far will you have traveled while you weren't looking?

One second is the absolute maximum length of time you should allow yourself to take your eyes off the road. If you're not sure how long that is, it's about the length of time it takes to say, at a normal speaking speed, "one-one-thousand." Not very long, that's for sure.

Obviously you shouldn't take your eyes off the road at all if you're in heavy traffic, or where there are stop signs and traffic lights, or children or other pedestrians, or generally wherever you need to pay extra close attention to what's going on around you.

If there's something you need to do in the car, pull over somewhere and stop.

A good strategy when you're doing something like tuning the radio is to flick your eyes constantly back to the road, so that you never really have it out of your view.

Because a lot can happen in a third of a football field.

And another thing: the distance your car will travel in an instant of inattention is a very good reason for not following closely. If you keep your distance from the car ahead, you'll have enough space to avoid a collision if the other car slows or stops unexpectedly.

Here's how to check that you're at a good "following distance": Watch as the rear bumper of the car ahead of you passes a specific point – a road sign, a mailbox, or anything else you can set for yourself as a marker. Count slowly until your front bumper reaches the same point. If you count, "one-one-thousand, two-one-thousand," that takes about two seconds. Two seconds of "following distance" should give you enough time to observe and react. But this rule goes for good driving conditions. In rain or snow or anything that makes stopping harder, you need more time/distance between you and the car ahead.

Ice and Snow

There are not many people who think driving on ice and snow is fun. Most of those are probably snow-mobile owners. The difference between a nice dry road and one with ice and snow on it is pretty major. Ignoring that difference could cost you bigtime!

But there are quite a few things you can do to drive safely in winter conditions. Here are some key ones, and they will probably sound pretty familiar:

Slow down. This is the first rule for getting where you're going instead of landing in a ditch.

Don't hold the steering wheel too tightly. This may sound counter-intuitive, but by holding the wheel gently, instead of gripping it for dear life, you'll be able to let the car readjust itself if it slides a little. Of course, if the car skids widely, you'll have to use the wheel to correct it. But the car will actually correct *itself* out of little slips as long as you're not preventing it from doing that by tightly gripping the wheel. Try it out sometime on an icy day in a large empty parking lot.

Use every bit of traction available. If the road is **icy**, there may be some rougher ice along the side of the road. That rough stuff gives you traction. So instead of driving in the wheel tracks of other cars, keep your right-side wheels in the area where the ice or snow is more lumpy and granular. The wheel tracks of previous cars are compacted and smoothed by the cars traveling in them and so are more slippery than the rest of the road. Under icy conditions, you're better off staying out of them as much as you can.

But, on the other hand, if the road is covered with *slushy* snow, you are instead *safer* in the tracks made by other cars. Under slushy conditions, the tires of previous vehicles will have moved the slush out of the way, leaving clearer tracks. On the sides of the road, there will be deeper slush that you don't want to get into.

In short, you need to choose how to travel on snowy, icy, or slushy roads by gauging where you will have the most traction.

Avoid using your brakes. On ice, even if your vehicle has anti-lock brakes, don't use the brakes if you can possibly avoid it. If you're coming up on a stop sign or a red light, take your foot off the gas and let the car slow gradually to a halt. If you're going around a curve or making a turn, slow down before you get to it by taking your foot off the gas. If necessary, apply the brakes in short, light taps, leaving time between the taps for the car to regain traction.

Braking, especially sudden braking, can cause your car to skid in icy or snowy conditions, so keep about twice the distance you usually do between you and the car ahead.

Another thing--you're more likely to skid going downhill than going uphill, even if you don't use your brakes. So be alert to that possibility and go slow as you come over the crest of a hill, or turn onto a street going downhill.

And if you can, take a less hilly route than usual to your destination.

Here are some more tips for winter weather driving:

In a manual transmission (stick shift) car, don't use the engine (by shifting into a lower gear) to slow the car, unless you do it gradually or unless the car is already moving pretty slowly. If you're going along fairly fast and suddenly shift into a lower gear in order to slow down, the car will reduce speed abruptly. This will have much the same effect as if you slammed on the brakes, and it is just likely to cause a skid. Instead, disengage the engine by pushing in the clutch. This lets the car slow gradually and smoothly. And gradual and smooth are what you're looking for when driving on ice and snow.

Don't speed up abruptly. When you suddenly speed up, you're calling on greater traction for the tires. If there's snow and ice on the road, that traction isn't there and the car may skid.

Drive smoothly and steadily. Avoid quick motions or turns. The car has a much better chance of moving along without skidding if it's going at a steady rate.

Watch out on bridges and overpasses. "Watch for ice on bridge." "Bridge freezes before road surface." These signs look funny in the summer, but they're not so funny in the winter. Since there's air under a bridge or overpass, the road surface there is a good deal colder than it is where the road runs over solid ground. The colder surface means that when temperatures are near freezing, any puddles, rain, or drizzle will freeze on the bridge or overpass sooner than it will on other parts of the road. So although you were driving along on a road that was only wet, you may suddenly find yourself on an icy bridge. The moral of the story? If the air temperature is close to freezing, be alert and slow down when you come to bridges and overpasses.

Beware of black ice. Black ice is an awful driving condition. It happens when light rain or mist freezes on the road surface in such a thin sheet that you can't even see it. The road ahead just looks its normal black or dark gray color. You might not have any idea at all that you're on black ice until you try to apply your brakes and nothing happens—the car doesn't slow down! So if there's light rain or mist in the air and the temperature is dropping out of the low 30s into the 20s, beware that black ice may be forming. Black ice is really, really slippery, and the safest thing is to get off the road altogether and wait until conditions get better.

If you have four-wheel drive or all-wheel drive, you do have some advantage on snow, especially if there's more than an inch or so – but don't overdo that idea and think you can still drive as though the pavement was dry! If there's snow on the road, slow down. And don't count on four-wheel drive to help you on ice, because on ice traction can be pretty much zero no matter what kind of vehicle you have.

Flowing Water

Flowing water has amazing power. A gallon of water weighs 8.35 pounds. When a stream flows over a road way, thousands of gallons of water can be passing by every second. As Captain Bob Gunderson of the Los Angeles Fire Department writes in his article, "Swift Water Rescue," water moving at 10 miles per hour exerts a force of 400 pounds per square inch on an object in the water – your car, for example. This is so much pressure that at a depth of a mere 10 inches, flowing water can carry away a small car. It takes a depth of about 14 inches to do that to a large sedan, as described in the 2003 Discovery Channel program, "The Power of Water."

Add to this the fact that when you're looking at water flowing over a road, it's very hard – or even impossible – to tell how deep it is. If there's a dip in the road, the water flowing across it will have a flat surface that conceals the dip. What looks like a couple of inches may be a few feet in depth in the middle of the dip, and you wouldn't even know it.

If you come across a place where water is flowing across the road, especially if it's a stream in flood, the smart thing to do is turn around and get to your destination by another road. If you drive into flowing water, it could send you on a big detour of its own.

Hydroplaning

Hydroplaning sounds like fun, and it is fun if you're in a hydroplane. It's not so fun if you're in a car.

If you see cars ahead of you sending up a lot of spray, this is a good indication that conditions are ripe for hydroplaning. Hydroplaning can happen whenever there's a film of water on the road, such as during a heavy rain, or if there's shallow water flowing across the road or a shallow pool of water on the road.

If you're going fast through standing water, your tires do not have enough time to push the water out to the sides as they travel through it. Instead, water will build up between your tires and the road. Then you will have no traction at all. Zip. Nada. You'll be hydroplaning.

How do you know if you're beginning to hydroplane? You may feel the car's back end slewing a bit from side to side. Or the steering may feel suddenly loose.

What do you do if you start hydroplaning? First of all, *don't touch the brakes.* This is the worst thing you can do. Instead, *take your foot off the gas* so the car will slow by itself. Second, *steer straight ahead* – don't try to turn in any direction. Even four-wheel drive will not help at all in this situation. In short, the best thing to do – in fact it's the only thing you should do – is allow the car to slow down enough that the tires regain contact with the road. (Check out the SUV Internet Training Center, www.suvone.com.)

So how do you avoid hydroplaning? Speed is the main thing that leads to hydroplaning. If you're going 55 miles an hour, there's a really good chance that your car will hydroplane on a very wet road. Even 45 or 35 could be too fast. So if you see that the road ahead looks really wet, not just damp, or if it becomes wet in a downpour, for example, slow down before you get into trouble. Slower speeds will give your tires time to push the water away.

Tire pressure also has an effect – low tire pressure increases the likelihood of hydroplaning. The kind of tread on your tires makes a difference, too. Some treads work better to siphon water off to the sides and away. Consider this issue when you go to buy new tires.

No Hilltop Surprises

You're heading up toward the top of a hill on a two-lane road. It's a narrow road, or maybe a residential street, and has no white line in the middle to separate the lanes. You've been driving along not quite all the way over on your side of the road, since there hasn't been anyone else on that road, at least not near you.

But now, invisible, climbing the hill toward you from the other side, is another car. The driver also has not been paying too much attention to staying over on her side so you are both pretty much in the middle of the road as you reach the top of the hill. And the conclusion of this scenario? It's one that happens fairly often on smaller roads everywhere, especially out in the country.

So it's a good idea to make it a rule to be well over in your lane whenever you're going up a hill. If the road is narrow, less than full two lanes wide, get *way* over and slow down. That way you won't have any hilltop surprises, even if a driver coming your way is hogging the middle.

And you if happen to be way out in the country and the road is really only one or one-and-a-half lanes wide, honk your horn as you get near the top of the hill and slow *way* down.

All this also holds true for sharp curves. (Think of a sharp curve as a hill lying on its side.) If you're going around a sharp curve and can't see what's coming from the other direction – there are trees in the way, for example – keep well to the right. *Definitely* do not cross the center line, if there is a center line, or drive in the middle of the road if there isn't. Then you won't have any curve surprises either.

Signaling

The purpose of signaling is to let drivers behind you know that you're going to slow down and turn off the road.

This is obvious. But the thing to remember is to let the other drivers know far enough in advance that the information actually does them some good. There's no point in signaling as you're in the act of making the turn. By then they already can see that you're turning--but you haven't given them a chance to be prepared.

How far in advance is far enough? You don't want to make it so far in advance that the driver behind you just thinks you've forgotten your turn signal is on. And of course the speed you're going makes a difference. A good rule of thumb is half a block in city or town driving, and about 100 yards on a highway. But check your state's driver's education manual, which will give you the exact recommended distance.

If You're Going to Turn, Turn

Some drivers seem to think that a car is designed along the lines of a bicycle. With that misconception in mind, they make hugely wide turns. This is why you sometimes see people pulling well to the left in preparation for making a right-hand turn.

This procedure is totally unnecessary. A car is not a bicycle and it can make much sharper turns primarily because it has four wheels, not just two. Making this leftward loop before a right turn is not only unnecessary but confusing to drivers behind. To turn right, just turn right.

Another habit to avoid is a long-drawn-out slowing down before making the turn, and then creeping around it. Obviously you need to slow down before turning, but not to a crawl. The turn should be made at a reasonable speed, unless of course there's something in the way, such as a pedestrian. What you want to avoid is leaving the rear end of your car hanging out for a prolonged time in the lane of traffic. This is hazardous to drivers behind you, who rightfully expect that after you've signaled and begun to turn, you will make the turn at a normal speed and get out of their way.

Especially if you're on a highway where cars are moving at speed and you want to make a right turn onto a side road, it's really key to move over as much as possible toward the shoulder as you slow down for the turn (not to mention signaling in advance). Under highway conditions, slowing too much while you're still in the lane makes you a major danger to drivers coming behind you--and puts you at risk, too.

Intersections: Whose Turn Is It?

Here you are sitting at a stop sign at a four-way intersection. Another driver, on the street that crosses yours, has arrived at the same time as you and is now also sitting at a stop sign. So who goes first?

Short of waiting for the stop-sign to turn green, since it won't, it's helpful to know the highway protocol.

The primary general rule is that the car that arrived first goes first.

This rule doesn't help, though, if everybody happens to arrive at the same time. On such occasions, a secondary rule comes into play. The secondary rule gives the right of way to a car on your right. Or to you, if you are on the other driver's right.

So if the other driver on the cross-street is on your right, *she* has the right of way. You wait. But if the other driver is on your left, *you* have the right of way (because you are on *her* right.) So you get to go first. But don't forget that the other driver may not be aware of this protocol, so don't just charge forward.

Here's another confusing scenario. You're going along on a two-way street and you come to a stop sign at an intersection. There's a stop sign on the other side, too, for cars coming from the other direction. You want to turn right onto the cross-street. A car opposite you also wants to turn onto the cross-street going in the same direction as you (you can tell from the car's turn signal—assuming the driver bothers to use it). You've both arrived at the stop signs at the same time. So who has the right of way?

The general rule here and in all similar situations is that if you're turning right, and therefore *not crossing a lane of traffic* on the road you're turning onto, you have the right of way. The opposite car, turning left, *will* be crossing a lane of traffic on the cross-street (in order to get into the correct lane) and therefore does not have the right of way over you. You get to go first.

Again, it's worth keeping in mind that other drivers may not know these rules. If a lot of hesitation is going on, the safest solution is to wait until

someone else goes. Or you could just to wave the other driver through if he
seems to be dithering.

Right Turn on Red

A right turn at a red light has been permitted in all 50 states for a bunch of years. At intersections where this is *not* permitted, there will be a sign to indicate that.

So when you're at a red light and want to turn right, you can do so, provided that (1) you first come to a stop, (2) there's no sign saying you can't, (3) there's no car coming on the cross street from your left, and (4) there's no pedestrian, bicycle, or vehicle in your way. According to research in several states, a third of all accidents resulting from a car turning right on red involve pedestrians (National Highway Traffic Safety Administration Report to Congress, February 1995). So this is an extra important place to watch out for pedestrians.

Because you're allowed to turn right on red when there's nothing to prevent you, a driver behind you is going to expect you to turn if you're sitting there at the light with your right turn signal on. So go ahead and turn if there's no reason not to!

Left Turn on Green

Say you're stopped at a red light and you want to turn *left*. You can't do that while the light is red (except in some states if the streets are both one way), but you can turn left when the light changes to green, as long as there's no one coming. And if there's a green arrow, as there is at many intersections, then it's obvious that you can turn when the green "left-turn" arrow lights up.

But supposing there's no green left-turn arrow and oncoming traffic (coming towards you on your same road through the green light) is in the way? The oncoming traffic has the right of way, natch, so you have to wait for those cars to pass before you make your left turn.

That all makes sense, right? But a lot of drivers aren't sure exactly where they should be while they're waiting for the traffic to clear. Should they stay back at the stop-line as though the light were still red, and wait there until traffic clears? *Not* the best idea. You don't have to stay back at the stop-line while you're waiting for oncoming traffic to go by. If there's a lot of traffic, you could be there all day, through change after change of the light! Infuriated drivers behind you will soon be honking and yelling.

Instead, move straight ahead into the intersection when the light is green. Be careful to stay within your lane. Wait in the middle of the intersection for the oncoming traffic to clear, and then turn. This is entirely legal and is the right course of action.

But what if the light turns red while you're still sitting there in the middle of the intersection? This is *still* okay, and you're *still* within your rights to be there because the light was green when you entered the intersection. So go ahead and make your left turn – but first make sure

that no oncoming car is going to barrel through the red light. Wait until oncoming cars have stopped.

Summing up: It's fine to enter an intersection on a green light and wait there for the traffic to clear before you turn left. It's still okay if the light happens to turn red while you're waiting in the intersection. Just turn when you can and when it's safe.

Negotiating Roundabouts

Roundabouts are very common in Great Britain and across Europe, and elsewhere too, but less so in the U.S.

In case you're not sure what a roundabout is, it's a fairly small, one-way, circular section of roadway at an intersection. It makes stop signs unnecessary. It's great for traffic flow.

At the roundabout, there will be a Yield sign instead of a Stop sign. Cars *already on the roundabout* have the right of way over cars entering the roundabout.

Look to your left as you approach the roundabout. All traffic will be coming from your left on this one-way circle (unless you're in the British Isles, where they drive on the other side of the road, but never mind about that now). As you already know to do at Yield signs, if there's traffic coming on the roundabout, stop. But if the way is clear, you don't have to stop – in fact, you shouldn't stop. Just head out into the roundabout, going to the right. Keep going around to the right until you get to the road you want to turn onto, and signal before turning.

Roundabouts are handy if you happen to miss your turn, since you can keep going around until you come to the street you want.

The Curvaceous Road

Probably you've seen television ads for sports cars that show the car dashing along a winding road. The driver of the car in the ad is always overjoyed at the winding road – the more curves the better!

Some of these ads should probably say, "Don't try this at home." Go too fast around a curve and you may find your car flying off at a tangent, no matter how great a sports car it is.

The problem of flying off a curve comes to us courtesy of the laws of physics – in particular the feature called *centrifugal force*. That's the same law a discus thrower uses when he spins around and around then lets go of the discus so that it hurtles away.

Fortunately, there's a good way to make this law of physics work *for* you instead of against you. You can do this by varying your speed in order to move into and pull smoothly out of the curve.

Here's how it works: First, as you're approaching and coming into the curve, slow the car down. You ought to be going at a reasonable speed for the road anyway, duh, so that preferably you can slow down by taking your foot off the gas, rather than braking..

If the curve is a really tight one, such as you might find on a very curvy rural road, keep your foot off the gas. Just as you pass the top of the curve and begin to come out of it, reapply the gas and speed up gradually, pulling smoothly out of the curve.

If the curve is not particularly tight, more of a relaxed loop, once you've slowed down you can gently reapply the gas while you're entering the curve to maintain a safe constant speed through the turn. This helps the car keep good traction on the road.

Recap: Slow down before the curve. Maintain a constant speed through the curve. Speed up smoothly coming out of the curve.

Driving winding roads through the countryside can be fun – as long as you keep the laws of physics on your side.

Braking

Here's a good rule of thumb: The less often you have to use your brakes, the better.

Try relying on the engine itself to slow the car down. As often as possible, just take your foot off the gas pedal when you need to slow – the drag of the engine acts like a brake.

Obviously you need brakes to come to a complete stop, but you can still ease into the stop by taking your foot off the gas in advance, and just use the brakes as you get to the stopping point. If you roar up to a stop sign and brake at the last minute, you're liable to give heart-failure to people driving on the cross-street.

Another thing you want to avoid, that relates to braking, is following another vehicle too closely. The reasons have to do with both reaction time (yours) and braking time (the car's).

On average, it takes three-quarters of a second to perceive and react to the need to stop, plus almost as long to move your foot from the gas pedal to the brake, for a total of about one and a half seconds. These figures come from many scientific studies and are included in a chart published by the traffic accident reconstruction firm Shepston & Associates.

In one and a half seconds, a car going 60 miles per hour will travel about 132 feet, or 44 yards – almost half the length of a football field. You've gone that far before you've even pushed down on the brake pedal!

After you put on the brakes, the car is still going to go a long way before it actually stops. On a dry road, at 60 miles per hour, the braking distance for a passenger car is about 172 feet. Putting together the perception/reaction time and the braking distance, the car goes over 300 feet before it comes to a complete stop. That's the entire football field right there.

And on a wet road? Add another 75 feet. On a snowy road? You're already in trouble if you're doing anything like 60 on a snowy road.

But supposing you're not on a highway, you're just driving through town, going along at the usual urban speed limit of 30 miles per hour

– that's 44 feet per second. Even now, by the time you've perceived and reacted to the need to stop and slammed on the brakes, your car's still going to travel a hundred feet, or 33 yards, before it stops.

One thing you might have noticed here: a car going 30 miles per hour takes 33 yards to stop, but a car going twice as fast, 60 miles per hour, takes 100 yards to stop. Twice the speed, but *more than twice as far*. In fact, this holds true up and down the speedometer. A car going 40 takes *more* than twice as far to stop as when it's going 20, and so on.

The faster you go, the harder it gets to stop. Those laws of physics are at work on the momentum of the car. Keep them on your side by going at speeds that will let you stop safely when you need to. Hey, you'll still get where you're going.

Seatbelts: What They're There For

It would be weird to find a race-car driver who didn't bother wearing a seatbelt. Seatbelts aren't just for sissies.

So you'd think everyone would just go ahead and wear one. After all, it's currently the law in 49 states (as of 2011, all states except New Hampshire), and in Washington D.C., Puerto Rico, and all the U.S. territories. But in fact the National Highway Transportation Safety Administration has found (see www.nhtsa.dot.gov) that only 7 out of 10 people in the U.S. – drivers and passengers – regularly wear a seatbelt.

That's really sad because look at what can happen if you don't. If you're going, say, 30 miles per hour and your car hits a tree, the car stops, but without seatbelts you and your passengers keep going at the same 30 miles per hour before crashing into the inside of the car – the steering wheel, the windshield, the dashboard, the back of the front seat. Think about the fact that for a child who's not wearing a seatbelt, a 30 mile-an-hour crash is like being dropped out of a third-story window.

Even with an air-bag, you're not okay without your seat belt. You'll still be moving forward when the car stops, and you then you'll be so close to the air bag that it could injure you pretty badly. Air bags come out of their housing with great force, deploying at between 165 and 210 miles per hour, as noted by Arthur Croft, www.chiroweb.com.

Especially in a roll-over or a crash where the car spins hard, without a seatbelt you have at least a 25 percent chance of being thrown out of the vehicle. You are no match for the laws of physics! Getting ejected from a vehicle is one of the worst things that can happen to you. It gives you a 75 percent chance of never going home.

Besides the fact that a seatbelt can save your life (and maybe someday it will), it also helps you stay in control of the car—something that's pretty crucial! Suppose you have to swerve hard to avoid something. Without a seatbelt, your body is going to be swung around as the car is swerving, making it super hard to handle the car. But with a seatbelt, which holds you firmly, you can stay steady while you're using the wheel. You have control.

Race car drivers wear seatbelts. They have lots of reasons. So do you.

Blinding Headlights

The night is dark, the road is narrow, and along comes a car from the other direction with its high beams on. The glare is mucho bright and right in your eyes.

So what should you do?

(A) Should you put on *your* high beams to pay the idiot back?

Bad idea!

(B) Should you flick your high beams on and off to alert the other driver to lower her headlights?

This is okay of you flick the high beams on very briefly, and only once. Flicking them repeatedly, let alone giving a long on-flick, is about as bad as (A).

A brief flick of your brights can remind the oncoming driver to lower her headlights, if she has just not remembered they're on high. That will work, and you can both travel past each other in safety.

But if a brief flick doesn't work, don't press the point. Because when you put on your high beams, either flicking them repeatedly or leaving them on, this creates a situation with *two* half-blinded drivers instead of only one.

(C) Here's the answer from the back of the book: If someone is coming toward you with headlights on high, and doesn't respond when you flick your lights briefly, do this: Shift your gaze to the edge of the road, the shoulder, on your right, a few yards ahead of your car. Keep looking at the shoulder until you've passed the oncoming car.

This strategy lets you see where you're going because you're watching the side of the road ahead of you, but at the same time it keeps your eyes from being blinded by the oncoming headlights.

It's a safety factor, not just a courtesy, to lower your headlights when another car is coming toward you. In fact, you should lower them quite some distance in advance, about when you first see the lights of the other car approaching you, unless it's really far away.

If you're on a hilly road, you might not see an approaching car's headlights until the car is really close to you. But usually there are trees or telephone lines along the sides of the road and you can see the light from the headlights reflecting off them, even when you can't see the car yet. The reflection is a cue to lower your beams far enough in advance. And when you're following another car, remember that your headlights reflect glaringly in the driver's rear-view mirror – especially your high beams. So lower your headlights when you're behind someone, too.

Snails and Speed-Demons

Driving too fast can be dangerous. More accurately, it *is* dangerous. We all know that. Driving too fast – for the neighborhood, for the road, for the weather conditions, for the abilities of the car or the abilities of the driver – causes a great many accidents, injuries, and fatalities every day. Not to mention traffic tickets.

It's also true, however, that driving too *slowly* is dangerous. If you're driving significantly below the speed limit – and certainly if you do that routinely – you are a hazard for other cars on the road, in particular the ones behind you. If, for example, you're continuously going along at 20 in a 40-mile-per-hour zone, drivers behind you may become so frustrated they try to pass you at bad places. If there's a reason you have to be going slowly and you see cars lining up behind you, pull over so they can pass.

Or say you're on a highway where the speed limit is 55 and you're only going 45. Drivers coming up on your tail will reasonably assume that you're going somewhere near the speed limit. They may not notice, or they may not be able to tell, that you're going so slowly until they're right behind you and have to brake hard or swing around you – assuming they can do either of those things in time. You can cause an accident by going too fast. You can also cause an accident by going too slow.

This relates to the question of passing lanes on a highway, too. The passing lane is for passing other cars when necessary, or for when you have to turn left onto a side road. It's not for just driving along. Especially it's not for driving along too slowly.

Neither a snail nor a speed-demon be. Stick to a happy medium, which – weather permitting – is usually around the speed limit.

Road Rage and How to Beat It

It's easy to get mad at a driver who's bumbling along ahead of you when you're trying to get somewhere, or when someone cuts you off in traffic. Even if you're a generally mild-mannered person your irritation can escalate, especially if you're already worried about something else such as being late to wherever you're going.

How do you prevent that from happening? How do you get a handle on road rage before it starts?

Say you're driving along and there's a couple in the car ahead of you, going way below the speed limit. Whenever there's a bend in the road their car slows down even further. You've got a class, or a meeting at work first thing. You're already late! Your teacher or your boss is going to make comments. You get madder and madder at the faceless, nameless driver in front of you who's messing up your day. You're clenching your teeth and muttering, "Come on! Move it!"

The point here about "faceless and nameless" is that the other driver is most likely totally unknown to you. It's a whole lot easier to be angry at a silhouette with no identity, than at someone you know something about.   After all, when it gets right down to it, you have no idea what's making this person drive so slowly. If you did, you might not be so mad.

Maybe there's actually a good reason. Maybe the driver is taking her husband to the hospital for tests and the car-ride is making him feel sick. Maybe the driver is going to get his car fixed because there's something radically wrong with his brakes and he's scared about not being able to stop. Maybe the driver is looking for her dog that got out of the yard.

If you find yourself getting seriously irritated at another driver, before the frustration escalates try using your imagination to take away the "faceless, nameless" quality of that person. Imagining reasons *why* the other driver might be dithering along ahead of you can help you keep your cool.

And that driver who just cut you off, forcing you to hit your brakes? Well, relax—you're the better driver.

Alcohol

Do you need to hear any more statistics about drunk driving? Maybe, if you don't want to become one.

Alcohol reduces judgment and reaction time by a whole lot. If you've had too much to drink, you're no longer a good driver. In fact, your driving ability is already affected even before you can tell – or anyone around you can tell – that you've had too much to drink.

It takes guts to overcome your pride and let someone who's sober drive, or to take a taxi, or to call a friend or family member, or your mother! But you'll get home. You won't hurt or kill someone on the way. You won't hurt or kill yourself or wreck your car or get arrested. And that will feel infinitely better than wishing afterward that you hadn't gotten behind the wheel – and not being able to turn back the clock. Say you're embarrassed to call your mom or dad or your brother or sister to come get you. They'll yell at you for drinking. But what would they say if you passed up that idea and got in an accident and there you are in the hospital? "Why didn't you call me??" That's what they'd say.

Here are a couple of statistics from the National Highway Transportation Safety Administration:

Impaired driving is the leading cause of death for people under 30.

Drunk driving caused 40% of all fatal accidents in 2001, and led to 16,652 deaths. That's an awful lot of people who died unnecessarily. Drunk driving accidents are completely preventable.

Other things you've probably already heard – but hear them again:

Don't let someone else drive drunk – get hold of those keys.

Don't get into a car with a drunk driver – you'd be putting your life in real danger. Make an excuse, any excuse, not to. Or just tell it like it is.

And if you're out on the road and you see someone driving erratically, get out of the way. If they're behind you, turn off or pull over. If they're ahead of you, stay back. And if they're coming toward you, get well over on your side of the road, or turn off if you can. Take evasive action.

If You're Stopped by Police

Oh no. That siren behind is actually for you! Red and blue lights are flashing in your rear-view mirror. Ye gods, what now? Got to slow down, pull over, stop.

So how do you handle this unnerving situation?

Maybe you were going rather a lot over the speed limit. Maybe you thought that yellow light was going to last a little longer before it turned red, or you didn't quite see the stop sign in time. Or you're not wearing your seatbelt. Or maybe you really have no idea why you've been stopped (a tail light is out? your license plate fell off?)

First and foremost, the golden rule is, be polite. There's just no use handling it any other way.

If you know what you did wrong, say so. ("I'm sorry, Officer, I know I was going too fast." "I didn't see that stop sign in time; I should have been more careful." "I didn't realize the light was going to change so quickly." "I know I ran that light; I'm sorry." "I know I need to be wearing my seatbelt.") Or if you don't know, ask. ("Hello, Officer. What's wrong?") Courtesy is not wasted in these situations, not hardly.

Provide your license and car registration and answer any questions with good grace.

Keep your hands in sight.

Don't get out of the car unless you're asked to.

If you're in a city, especially after dark, absolutely do *not* pull into an alley, even to get out of the way of traffic. Your pulling into an alley can be alarming to the officer. Remember, police pretty much take their lives in their hands when they make traffic stops.

If you're being stopped in a deserted or unlit area, it's a very good idea and perfectly okay to continue to drive on *slowly* until you come to more populated place, a gas station, a convenience store, somewhere where there are lights and people. If you're stopped by an someone you think is a police officer, but who's out of uniform and in an unmarked car, this could be a sign of someone impersonating an officer. Don't open your window more than a crack, and ask for identification. (Check out "The Traffic Stop and You," Bloomington, Indiana, Police Department, 2003.)

When Something Goes Wrong

You're on a major highway and your car breaks down – everybody's nightmare. You manage to pull over into the break-down lane or onto the shoulder and come to a stop. Safe for the moment! Now what?

Here's what: Stay in the car. Lock the doors. Don't leave any window open more than a couple of inches. If you have a cell phone, call 911, or AAA if you're a member, or a towing service if you know of one nearby.

If you don't have a cell phone with you, wait for the police.

Suppose someone (other than a police officer) stops to help you. Or offers you a ride to the nearest garage. Do you go? No, no, and no! No longer can you get into a car with a stranger and have a good chance of being safe. Those days went out with "Leave it to Beaver."

If you don't have a cell phone with you and a stranger stops to help, ask the stranger (not opening the window far enough for him to get a hand through) to call 911 for you. Then wait till official help comes.

Even on a country road at midnight, when you think help will be a long time in coming, you're still safest if you stay in your car. This kind of situation makes a cell phone a life-saver. Don't leave home without it. (But don't text on it while you're driving!)

Above all, as you were probably told in childhood, don't *ever* get in a car with a stranger. That's a very big risk. Way too big.

Don't Be a Victim

Someone driving alone, especially a woman, can be a target for of criminals. Say you're driving after dark on a little-traveled road or even a highway and another car starts following you. The car pulls up next to you and the driver shouts at you to pull over. There's something wrong with your car, he yells. Oil is leaking! Gas is leaking! You have a flat tire! The rear end is about to fall off! Lady, pull over!

DON'T pull over. This is very likely a trick, even if the guy looks perfectly nice (it doesn't matter how nice he looks). Speed up. Drive out of that situation if you possibly can. Get to a populated area. Find a gas station that's open and then check your car if you're concerned.

Suppose you can't drive out of the situation. He pretty much forces you off the road. He comes to the driver's side window, looking pleasant. "Lady, get out. You should look at this. You've got a lot of gas leaking out of the back of your car."

DON'T get out. Lock all the doors. Leave the windows rolled up. If possible, now that he's out of his car, start up and drive off fast. Get out of there. If you have a cell phone with you, call 911. If you can't get out of there, start blowing the horn like mad. Do *not* be a victim. Do everything you can to protect yourself.

Getting out of deep water

You slid off the road and your car has gone into a pond, a lake, a river, the ocean near the road and it's sinking. This is one of the most terrifying things that can happen, and definitely one of the most dangerous. But it's survivable if you know what to do.

So let's take a look at what you need to know to stay calm and get out of this really bad situation if it should happen to you.

When you see that you're going into the water, brace yourself with your hands on the steering wheel so that when the airbag goes off – if your car is equipped with one—you'll be far enough away from it that it won't hit you as hard as it would otherwise.

Absolutely *do not* try to call someone for help on your cell phone!! *You* must get *yourself* out because only you can do that in time. And you can. If the water is deeper than the height of the car, you will have between one and three minutes, and that's enough time.

First, unbuckle you seatbelt so you're free to move. If there are passengers in the car, make sure one of them is unbuckled who can then help others.

Now, immediately try to open the driver's side window. The car's electronics should continue to function for at least two minutes in the water. *Do not* try to open the door. As the car sinks, the weight of the water outside will make it impossible to open the door and you will lose valuable time trying to do that.

If the window doesn't open or opens only part way, you'll have to break it (you can very probably break a side window, but don't try breaking the windshield; it's way too thick). If you have any kind of tool, use it—a screw driver, an umbrella, a high-heeled shoe, a camera, or certainly a hammer if you have one. In fact, if you routinely drive near bodies of water it's a really good idea to keep a small hammer within reach of the driver's seat, or you can get one of the tools designed for escaping from a car at a hardware or auto parts store. Aim at the center of the window and hit as hard as you can.

If you don't have a tool or hard object, use your feet. In this case, aim at either the front edge or the door-hinge edge of the window--these are the weaker points--or at the top of the window if you've been able to open it part way. Take a deep breath, pull yourself out, and swim to the surface.

If you aren't able to open or break the window, within two or three minutes the car will fill with water as it sinks. Keep your head in an air space for as long as you can and breathe as calmly as you can. Keep your hand on the door handle so you don't lose track of where it is. When the water pressure equalizes between the outside of the car and the inside, you'll be able to open the door and get out.

Remember, you can get out. You need to be ready with the knowledge of how to do that.

Short-Takes

How you hold the wheel

Some books on driving suggest holding the steering wheel in the "ten o'clock and two o'clock" position -- that is, with your hands down from the top of the wheel on each side. This position can provide stability especially under tough driving conditions, say on a winding road, or in bad weather. It's fine if it works for you. But with the excellent power steering of today's cars, another position now recommended **for highway driving** is to hold the wheel in a "five o'clock and seven o'clock" position, with palms up and thumbs hooked over the wheel. This position allows you to use just your wrists to control the wheel.

There are other possibilities that also work well. One is the "twelve o'clock and eight o'clock" position, where you have your right hand on the top of the wheel, doing most of the control, and your left hand at the eight-o'clock position to steady the wheel. Or, if you're left handed, or if it just feels more comfortable for you, put your left hand at the top of the wheel and your right hand at the four o'clock position.

The important thing is to find the position that is most comfortable for you and gives you the best sense of control, depending on the driving and road conditions.

When your lane is blocked

You're on a two-way suburban street and there's a delivery truck stopped right in your lane, taking up all the room. In order to get by it, you have to drive on the other side of the road. But remember, you don't have the right of way on that side of the road! If a car is coming toward you, that car has the right of way and you have to wait until there's no one coming to pull around the truck.

The invisible car

Here you are, about to turn onto a four-lane road. You want to go south, and so you've got to cross the two northbound lanes. A northbound van is approaching in the nearest lane and you wait for it to pass. It looks like that's the only vehicle coming from that direction. It passes and you're just about to pull out – but wait! There's a smaller car that was traveling in the further northbound lane, just a bit back of the van so that it was totally invisible from your angle of vision, completely hidden by the other vehicle.

This happens a lot. In this kind of situation, even when it looks like there's only one vehicle going by, wait to be sure there's no "invisible" car behind it.

Horn honking

The horn is a warning device. It's not meant for greetings. While you're honking your horn loudly and waving at your friend who's on the sidewalk or driving by, you may be startling nearby drivers, who automatically think you're warning them of something.

Parking lots

Parking lots are pretty lawless driving environments. Occasionally in a large lot there are stop signs here and there, but for the most part there's not much to control the flow of traffic. People can, and do, drive across parking lots in any direction. Pedestrians walk behind cars that are backing out. Cars back toward each other out of opposite spaces.

In parking lots you need eyes like a fly, alertly looking in every direction.

Blind-spot mirrors

There's a blind-spot in the area to the left of your car's rear bumper. The side mirror on the driver's side doesn't cover that space. A car can be coming up behind you in the lane to your left, ready to overtake and pass you, and when it gets to the blind-spot, you can't see it. You might look in your side mirror and think the way is clear to pull into the left lane. But it isn't.

The same thing goes for the right side of the car. There's also a blind-spot to the right of the car's rear bumper which is not covered by the side mirror on the passenger's side.

This problem is easy to fix. For a couple of dollars you can buy a pair of blind-spot mirrors at any auto parts store and other places that sell auto-related products. Blind-spot mirrors are small convex mirrors, either round or rectangular. They have a glue patch on the back and you stick them onto the lower outside corners of your side mirrors – the left lower corner of the driver's side mirror and the right lower corner of the passenger's side mirror. They give you a clear view back along the sides of the car. Presto! No more blind spots.

Get in the habit of checking in the blind-spot mirrors before you pull left or right into an adjacent lane. *But* –turn your head and take that one last quick look to confirm absolutely and totally that there's no car in the way. Check-and-double-check = no accident.

Pulling back after passing

You're driving on a four-lane, or larger, highway and the car ahead of you is going a little under the speed limit and you decide it's time to pass. So, checking in your left side mirror to make sure there's nothing coming up on your left (and using your blind-spot mirror and then turning your head too!), you pull into the left lane and pass the car.

But when is it safe to pull back in lane? How can you tell if you're far enough past the other car?

This is actually pretty easy to figure out. Check the rear view mirror (not a side mirror). When you can see, in the rear view mirror, the front tires of the car you've just passed in contact with the road, then you've got enough distance to pull safely back into the lane.

Deer whistles

Deer whistles are not to call deer--they're to keep them away! If you drive in a big city, you presumably don't need deer whistles. But if you drive on country roads or highways where deer may be lurking, ready to leap out in front of you, deer whistles are a great idea.

Of course, you don't have to blow the whistles yourself. They're attached – two of them – on the car's front bumper, one on each side. The air rushing into them as you drive along creates a high-pitched whistle that is virtually inaudible to humans, but apparently sounds horrible to deer.

It's true that there's no research, so far, on how well deer whistles work. There's no certainty that they will always and absolutely cause approaching deer to turn away from the road. But they cost just a few dollars in any auto parts store -- a lot less than fender repairs – and many drivers have reported seeing deer turn away as the car approached. Some companies whose drivers have to travel roads in deer country routinely have them on their cars and trucks.

Be prepared for worst-case scenarios. If you're in an area where there are deer, keep a sharp eye out. Pay attention to "Deer Crossing" signs -- they're there because deer are creatures of habit and tend to use the same paths. Remember, if you see one deer, chances are there are others nearby.

At night watch for the reflection from a deer's eyes, or a silhouette at the side of the road.

Dusk, nighttime, and dawn are the main times that deer are on the move looking for food, so watch out if you're driving then. Also, November is mating season and deer are very active and their minds are definitely on something other than cars.